Contents

Chapter One: The Mummy Love Triangle

Mummy Love Triangle

The Mummy Love Triangle Murder

When something crazy happens, it almost always happens in Florida. There have been some weird tales about crimes that happened in the Sunshine State. Many thought this was a recent development, something snapped in the residents and they decided to act out. The thought was criminals wanted attention and they get it by being bizarre.

Carl Tanzler was the ultimate Florida man. He emigrated from Germany and moved to Key West, Florida in the early 1930s. After a few years, he became a successful radiologist. Then he found the woman he would marry, Doris Schafer. They would go on to have two children together, Ayesha and Clarista.

Despite being married, he found himself having feelings for a younger woman. One who was very ill when they met.

In Sickness

Maria Elena Milagro de Hoyos had been diagnosed with tuberculosis when she met Tanzler. The disease was killing her slowly, despite everyone's best efforts to cure her. Unfortunately, nothing seemed to work. The young lady became sicker and sicker by the day.

Despite this, Tanzler became enamored of de Hoyos. He romanticized the relationship between them and soon began having an emotional affair with her. There is no evidence his feelings were returned by de Hoyos, in fact, many think she was too ill and sad about her own marriage breaking up to even contemplate having an extramarital with him.

That didn't stop the de Hoyos family from accepting Tanzler's offer to help with her medical expenses. The radiologist set up an X-Ray machine for her in the house. He would spend every day creating new concoctions. Each of the inventions came with the promise of saving the young woman's life.

The concoctions didn't work. de Hoyos died just after her 21st birthday. Everyone who loved her was devastated by the loss. Tanzler lost his mind and went into deep denial about her death. He believed their love was so deep that not even death would be able to keep them apart. A plan was forming in his brain, one that he believed was fail-proof.

He was going to bring her back from the dead.

In Love With A Mummy

Tanzler asked the de Hoyos family if he could pay for the funeral, a request they quickly granted. The family was hard-pressed for money and many of them were ill with tuberculosis. None of them thought twice about the offer or why he would make such a grand gesture. They were just grateful that he would do this for their loved one. The generosity from the faux doctor would extend a bit further and may not have been as charitable as it first appeared.

There was also the mausoleum Tanzler built to house his beloved Helen in. After she was buried there, he visited every single night without fail. He would stay there from the time the sun set until it rose again. At some point, he decided that his deceased girlfriend should come home with him.

Getting the body was easy. All Tanzler had to do was take the body from the mausoleum and put it in a wagon. He walked right out of the cemetery and made it all the to his house without ever being stopped. The body was put on the couch once they got inside the house, as the radiologist set about making sure the corpse was comfortable.

There were reports of the man and the mummy being seen dancing from the window. Some have even said they believe there was sexual activity between him and the dead body. His love was so deep for de Hoyos that her dead body was treated better than his real wife was. The wife he married seemed to have disappeared altogether during this time.

The Fix Is In

The body began falling apart while in the custody of Tanzler. This was something that he was ready for. Since he didn't let death take de Hoyos from him, he wasn't going to allow decomposition to take her away from him. There was a plan to keep her with him for as long as possible.

The corpse was stuffed with rags in order to keep the shape intact. Piano wire and hangers were used to hold the skeleton in place. Wax and other materials with the same consistency were used to replace the skin as it fell off. Glass balls replaced her eyes when they fell out of her head.

As the corpse became less human, the harder he worked to keep the memory of de Hoyos alive. He wanted the love he felt for her to flourish. There was no way he wanted to give her up yet. He was convinced he could bring her back from the dead because he thought her to be his soulmate.

His solution was to send the corpse into outer space.

Returned and Displayed

De Hoyos' sister finally heard about what was happening. Seven years after the body theft, the cops were called in. They surrounded Tanzler's house and fought their way in. Helen's body was retrieved and taken back to the cemetery. But not for long.

Someone thought it was a good idea to put de Hoyos' mangled corpse on display for the public to see. A funeral home in Key West welcomed more than 6,000 visitors who wanted to see what had happened. The family allowed this to happen for a few weeks until the returned the body to the mausoleum.

Tanzler never faced charges for stealing the corpse. By the time the body had been retrieved, the statute of limitations was up on any of the crimes he could have been charged with. Because public sentiment was on his side, even if he had been charged with one of the crimes he committed, it is not believed he would have been convicted.

Doris Tanzler returned to the home she shared with her husband after all of this was over. When he fell ill, she took care of him until he died in 1952. Some reports suggested he died in the arms of de Hoyos' corpse, he switched the bodies before the authorities took it away. He was true to her until the end, despite his wife's loving care.

Chapter Two: Devil Murder

Devil Murder

<u>The Devil Made Him Do It</u>

Who hasn't referred to their ex as a psycho? Calling an ex-lover names is a rite of passage, a way of getting over an ex. Maybe in an extreme case, an ex could be called the devil. Mostly it would be a facetious insult, a way to vent some rage about the broken relationship. It is a good way to release the anger and help one get over the anger. Sometimes a breakup is extreme and there are things one partner didn't know about the other like they are uber-religious or mentally ill.

The case of 60-year-old David Murdock killed his ex-girlfriend for religious reasons, is one of the more extreme examples. When he was arrested, he informed the police about the reason he killed his ex-girlfriend. He believed that she had been possessed by the devil and he felt it was his responsibility to get rid of the evil from his ex.

The relationship was anything but harmonious, even when Murdock and his ex were together.

On and Off Break Ups

Lisa Bunce and Murdock had a troubled relationship from the get-go. Rumors swirled that Murdock was very jealous and wanted to keep tabs on where his girlfriend was at all times. This led the pair to argue frequently and break up even more. After the breakups, they would make up and the cycle would start again.

After a particularly nasty fight, Bunce ended the relationship in 2018. She wanted a fresh start after the dramatic era of her life, so she moved to Ohio. This allowed her to get away from Murdock and start her life over. There was still a pull towards her Floridian roots, it was after all where she was from.

It was for that reason, she returned to Haines City in January 2019. She visited her best friend Sandra Andrews. The women were enjoying some time together before dinner when Murdock began texting Bunce. At first, the messages were ignored. After being bombarded with messages from her ex-boyfriend, Bunce decided to block his number. She thought this would be the end of him.

She was wrong. Dead wrong.

Found A Way To Even The Score

After Bunce blocked him, Murdock got very angry. He decided that it was up to him to find her and teach the woman he used to love a lesson. She was not acting the way he wanted or expected her to. In his mind, they were supposed to reconcile. Bunce was supposed to miss him so much that she begged him to take her back. It turned out that she didn't miss him at all and this was unacceptable to him.

Murdock did some investigating of his own and learned where Bunce was staying. He decided it would behoove him to go to see his ex in person. When he got there, Sandra Andrews answered the door to her house. She was surprised to see Murdock standing in front of her. He pushed himself into the house and started yelling for Bunce to show herself.

When he found her, an argument ensued. He produced a gun and shot her in the head twice. Then he stuffed her in a nearby closet. Police would find the body later, after being called by multiple people, including Murdock himself.

The murderer shot Andrews in the face.

Police found her barely conscious before the paramedics took her away, they asked who had shot her and Bunce. She reportedly answered "David."

Many people questioned why Murdock would kill a woman that he had proclaimed to love? The answer was simple, he did it for religious reasons.

Ridding The World Of Evil

It is not very often that religion or religious reasons are given for a person committing murder. Usually, there is a monetary motivation like life insurance or an inheritance. Or the killer is jealous that the one they loved has moved on to someone else. The reverse can often be used as well, a person wants to move on but their partner isn't interested in breaking up. Religion though seems to be a unique motivation that is only used on rare occasions.

According to Polk County Sheriff Grady Judd, Murdock confessed to the murder of Bunce and shooting Andrews in the face. He then told investigators that "he had to get rid of the devil." It seems as though he had found religion and believed his ex had been possessed by Lucifer. He took it upon himself to rid the world of evil. Plus, she wouldn't take him back and that really galled him.

Despite the defense, Judd promised that there was no way Murdock was going to get away with the crimes he committed. The sheriff told local reporters: "Lots of people blame the Devil for their misdeeds, but it takes a person to pull a trigger. We are going to hold Murdock accountable for murdering his ex-girlfriend and trying to kill another woman." To that end, a grand jury indicted him easily.

Murdock faces a lot of charges including; first-degree murder, attempted first-degree murder, armed burglary with assault/battery and shooting into a building. he is being held in the county jail without bond.

He stayed with his devil defense.

Chapter Three: Husband Hunting

Hunting Lover

<u>Husband Hunting, Lover Murders</u>

There are many stories about high school sweethearts getting married. Some of the stories are romantic and sweet, they serve as an inspiration to many. Other stories are cautionary tales about the perils of marrying too young. And then there's the Florida woman who decided to kill her husband because she wanted to build a life with their mutual friend, but she didn't want to do the deed herself. She persuaded her lover to kill her high school sweetheart, so she could keep her hands clean and collect the life insurance policy.

Denise and Mike Williams met when they were young children. They started dating when they were in high school. Many of their classmates and loved ones said they were the cutest couple in Florida. They tried to spend as much time as possible together. So when Mike took up duck hunting, his beloved girlfriend went along with him.

With every fairy tale though, there are obstacles to overcome. In this case, Denise decided that Mike was not her Prince Charming after all, and she was no Cinderella.

Cheating And Marriage

Shortly after Denise and Mike were wed, she began having an affair with their best friend, Brian Winchester. Neither Denise nor Brian felt guilty about betraying Mike. The two seemed to enjoy sneaking around and engaging in risky behavior that would almost get them caught. The arrangement suited the cheaters until it didn't any longer.

Denise tired of being married to Mike and thought it would be better if he died. To that end, she came up with a plan, Brian would kill her husband but only after there was a financial incentive for his death. Denise used seduction and guilt to get Mike to buy life insurance policies. She used their baby girl as part of her argument to buy the policies, then she asked him to make sure his favorite females were taken care of, if something happened. Finding no fault in the reasoning, Mike agreed and bought the insurance policies. He had no idea that he signed his own death warrant.

The plot was set in motion. Mike's days were numbered.

Alligator Feed Theory

After their daughter was born, Denise had stopped going on hunting trips with her husband. On December 16, 2000, Mike went duck hunting early in the morning. It was their wedding anniversary and the couple was supposed to celebrate. That was the plan.

The celebration that took place was not the one that had been planned between the married couple. Denise secretly celebrated when Mike never returned home. A search was started to try to find Mike, but there was very little evidence found. Some witnesses told investigators that they had saw Mike fighting with someone, but they didn't pay much attention since the people fighting were so far away. Mike must have fallen off the boat, hit his head and drown, police theorized. They added that it was likely alligators ate what they could from the body and the rest would turn up later.

This cleared Denise and Brian of any wrongdoing, or so they thought. Neither factored in one important part of the story: The mother-in-law.

The Relentless Mother-In-Law

To the public, Denise seemed to be the stereotypical widow. Investigators though revealed later that it was just an act.They never saw signs of her being the grieving widow. In fact, she seemed disinterested in anything relating to the investigation and never asked about the progress that was being made. They also noted that when the insurance money came in, Denise cheered up considerably. That wouldn't last though. Both Denise and Brian forgot Mike's mom.

Forgetting the mother-in-law? That's just bad murdering.

Mike's mother, Cheryl Ann Williams, was the opposite of her daughter-in-law. She called the police every day, sent them postcards, and generally just made sure they were looking for her little boy. Never once did she buy into the theory that alligators ate him. Some called it a mother's delusion but some people listened to her. They kept the investigation open at her behest.

Breaking Up Is Criminal To Do

It would be assumed that with Mike out of the picture, Brian and Denise would be happy and more in love than ever. That assumption would be wrong. They married and had a volatile relationship. Which was complicated by the Mike's sex addiction. He used the condition as the reason he cheated on Denise so often. After a while, she got sick of it and ended their relationship forever. This set her own downfall into motion.

Being dumped did not agree with Brian, especially by the woman he had loved for so long. One day, he climbed into her backseat and waited for her to get into the car. When she did, he held a gun to her head and forced her to start driving. While she drove, he let her know that if she saw the divorce through, he would make her pay for it. Fearing for her life, she pulled over in a CVS parking lot. She talked him down and convinced him to get out of the car. Then she called the police and filed a report. Like Mike before her, she sealed her own fate.

Brian was arrested and started to reveal what happened the day Mike was murdered.

Murderer Confesses The Truth

With Brian in jail, Denise must have felt confident about where her life was heading. Things must have seemed to have calmed down, her mother-in-law was busy bothering authorities trying to get more manpower to investigate Mike's death but no one was looking her way. Oh, how wrong she was.

While the black widow was celebrating, her estranged husband was busy with the police. He cut a deal with the police. In exchange for lesser charges, he would tell them exactly what happened to Mike Williams. They agreed. He revealed that Denise had coerced him into killing her husband when he went on his duck hunting trip. He and Mike had argued, resulting in a physical fight. What was supposed to be an easy murder turned complicated when the victim fought back. Eventually Brian pulled the trigger and killed his one time best friend.

Police verified every detail he told them. Including where they would be able to find the body. With the new information and newly discovered body, they were able to bring the case to a close. They turned everything over to the prosecutors and to a grand jury. This resulted in Denise being charged with murder and insurance fraud.

Her attorney argued that she had done nothing wrong and Brian had been the one to pull the trigger. They questioned why he wasn't he being charged with anything in regards to the Mike Williams case. The deflection tactic did not work. Denise was convicted of conspiracy to commit murder, first-degree murder, and accessory after the fact. A Judge sentenced her to life in prison.

Is there any doubt she wishes there was another lover to take out her second husband?

Chapter Four: Hide And Go Murder

Hide and Go Murder

Hide And Go Murder

Keeping a relationship fresh is not always easy. There are multiple ways for a couple to keep the home fires burning. Vacations are a great way for a couple to spice up their sex life. Other couples chose to go a different way and become different people, at least for a night. Every couple has to make the choice for themselves. There generally is no wrong answer, but some people may take it too far.

One of those couples that allegedly took it too far is Sarah Boone and Jorge Torres, Jr. Allegedly is used because there is some doubt that Torres had any say about what happened. They allegedly played what was supposed to be a sexy game of hide and seek. However, one of them would not make it through the game alive. Which has led to police and other people wondering if there was a murder plot in place.

Did one partner really want the other dead that badly? It would appear that was the case.

The Innocent Mistake

Boone explained to the police that she and her boyfriend were playing an innocent game of hide and seek. During this game, Torres climbed into the luggage, which she admits to zipping up the bag. Some have pointed out that Torres showing his girlfriend where he was hiding was strange and against the rules of the game they were playing. Nevermind that Boone was drinking, and likely she was drunk during the game.

She then changed her story a bit and told the police that rather than this being a game, she thought it would be "funny" if Torres climbed into the luggage. Once again she admitted to zipping up the suitcase and added that she went upstairs to lay down. She forgot about her boyfriend being in the bag until she woke up the next morning and her cell phone was ringing. She did not say who was calling her. However, she ran downstairs to let him out of the bag. But it was too late, Torres had died.

To her credit, she called 911 right away and told them her boyfriend was unresponsive. Emergency services were sent out to her house right away.

The Murder Plot

Police have had a hard time buying that this was a deadly accident. Especially since her story kept changing from one interview to the next. However, investigators started seeing what they believe to be the real story when they first walked into the house. Which is why they have questioned Boone's "inconsistent" stories.

They took a look at Boone's cell and have determined that this was not a mistake and in fact seems as if it was premeditated murder. With that they have seen from the cell phone, Torres calls for his girlfriend to let him out. He can be heard saying he is having a hard time breathing. However, Boone doesn't seem to care about the discomfort her partner is feeling. In fact, it seems as though she is delighting in his pain. She is heard saying, "For everything you've done to me. Fuck you."

She is so angry with her boyfriend for some perceived slights against her. After another call of being unable to breath from Torres, Boone responds "Yeah, that's what you do when you choke me. Oh, that's what I feel like when you cheat on me..." That statement has led investigators to believe she meant for her beau to die in the suitcase. They believe her drinking and "forgetting" to let him out was a way for her to make it seem like this was an accident. It didn't work out the way she had hoped it would.

Boone was arrested and charged with second-degree murder.

Chapter Five: Revenge Porn

Revenge Porn

<u>Social Revenge Porn</u>

For better or worse, social media has changed communication. Some friends only speak through comments on sites like Facebook and Instagram. Or through direct messages on each of the sites. Social media has also changed the way people seek to get revenge on those they perceived to have wronged them.

Revenge wasn't so sweet for Jonathon Stokes. His ex-girlfriend wouldn't do a favor for him, so he decided to seek vengeance on her. Social media was the avenue he chose to get his revenge. Because of cyberharassment laws in Florida, Stokes broke the law with his actions.

Revenge Snap

It all started when Stokes was getting ready to go on vacation. He reached out to his ex-girlfriend to take care of his dogs. The ex will remain unnamed because of the nature of this Florida Man story. Almost every report has said that Stokes and his ex were on friendly terms, though outside of him asking for a favor there was no other evidence to support this claim. Though it is one of those things that could be true because he did ask for such a big favor.

Fur babies are treated like human children with a lot of people. Stokes was one of those people. While he was away, he would check in on them. There was something happening that he didn't like, though he never specified exactly what it was. All he said on the multiple social media posts that he made was that she wasn't caring for the puppies the way he wanted her to. His friends would comment, telling him to cool off and enjoy his vacation but that would not do for Stokes. He was mad.

When he got home, he vowed to get revenge on his ex. There was a video of him and his ex being intimate on his phone. As with many people, social media seemed to be the best way to get vengeance. To that end, he uploaded the video and sent it to a bunch of his buddies on Snapchat and also made the sex tape his Snap story. Since Snaps are supposed to disappear after 10 seconds, he must have thought that would be the end of it all. But as many people could have told him, Snaps don't disappear.

Snap Is Forever

As she gained notoriety, the ex was finally shown the sex tape by one of her friends. After being shown the video, she went to the police and made a complaint. Given the nature of her allegations, the cops took the report and investigated the claims.

When he was asked about the video, Stokes denied knowing about it and uploading it. Even as the cops were letting him know the video was uploaded from his Snapchat account. He was informed that even if his account had been hacked, the hacker would have needed access to the young man's phone in order to put the sex tape on the platform. He continued to deny that he had anything to do with the upload, even with those facts.

Police were leery but brought the ex back in for more questioning. She told the police that while she gave permission to be filmed having sex with her then-boyfriend, she would never have given permission to have the video uploaded. Being a porn star was not on her list of things that she wanted to do with her life.

Once again the police talked to Stokes about the situation. During the questioning this time, he confessed to uploading the video. He told the investigators he did it because his ex did not take care of his puppies the way he wanted her to while he was away. Would a jury convict him with that defense? Even with the knowledge that revenge porn is illegal.

Snap Charges

It was a no brainer that prosecutors charged with cyberharassment. He was released on $1,500 bail as he awaited his August 20, 2019 arraignment. He pleaded not guilty but gave no indication about what his defense would be. Many believed he was hoping that he would be offered a plea deal in exchange for changing his plea.

A plea deal was always unlikely because of Stokes' lengthy criminal record. In 2013, he had been charged with beating up an elderly person and faced another fighting charge. He was again charged with assault and resisting arrest in 2016. When he was arrested for the cyberharassment and revenge porn case, he did not appear to resist arrest, so he at least he didn't continue to add on to the charges he faced.

Using social media can be a great way to connect with friends. However, it might behoove people who make sex tapes to keep it private between the people involved and not upload it for their friends to see on the platforms of their choice.

Chapter Six: Porn Star Murder

To Murder A Porn Star

To Murder A Porn Star

Early in October 2018, headlines in the queer blogosphere exploded with the death of Kyle Dean at the age of 21. Many of the stories recounted his porn career and how he was gay-for-pay. Many speculated that when he wasn't performing, he was heterosexual, though no evidence was offered to prove this theory. There are many men who this could have been written about. However, the story was a little bit different when it came to Dean. It wasn't just his all American good looks or the way his body looked when he was naked. It was the persona he displayed, at least in the beginning of his career. He portrayed himself as a man who couldn't believe he was getting paid to have sex, even when it was a man he was filming with. His life was cut short. Leaving many to wonder if it was his own doing or was it murder?

Like many of his porn star colleagues, Dean used a stage name in order to protect his real identity. Brandon Jason Chrisan was the name he was given at birth and what most of his loved ones called him. When he wasn't working, Dean enjoyed playing sports, especially football. He also claimed to have won fourth place in an Adult Body Training competition. There was no evidence to back up this claim.

Taking It Off On Camera

Dean was hired to perform in his first pornographic scene just after he turned 18. The scene was a heterosexual story that saw him playing a jock that the cheerleader partner couldn't seem to resist. Because the clip was such a big hit, Dean started booking more scenes and saw his star rise in the industry. Suddenly the straight porn directors and producers stopped hiring him altogether.

As luck would have it, gay porn would embrace Dean. He was incredibly popular with gay men given his looks and willingness to have sex with men. It would be here that Dean would make the most money. While a top in a gay porn makes between $200-$300 per scene, higher tier stars are able to ask for more money. The good thing about Dean was that he was in demand, even fans were asking to have sex with him. Times were good for him, until they weren't.

Like many before and after him, Dean picked up a drug habit. Many porn stars, especially in recent years, have drug habits that consume their lives and wreck their careers. While noone is certain when his addiction started, it became noticable fairly quickly. In the beginning of his career, getting and maintaining an erection wasn't a problem for Dean, but it started becoming an issue for him. As the offers stopped coming in, he began asking his fans for some of the essentials and to buy him things on his Amazon wishlist.

Third Chance Caveat

Many gay men had fantasized about topping Dean. One gay porn producer decided to try and convince Dean to appear in more gay porn videos but this time he would be the bottom. Dean agreed eagerly. Some people wondered if it was because he needed the money or if he had been on the receiving end of sex before and didn't really mind it. What effect did this have on his addiction? Many men, no matter their sexual orientation, have admitted to wanting to try anal sex. However, in most cases it is them that would be the one penetrating and not the one who is penetrated. There is no doubt that it could have led to him questioning his own sexuality. It could have made him turn to self-medicating to get the thoughts about his sexual orientation out of his head. Some in the industry have also said that producers may have given him the drugs to loosen him up.

While many of the queer media enjoyed extra clicks on their blog after the intial reports of his death, they dropped the story altogether. There could have been nothing more to report but that seems unlikely. However, there is always another twink or another jock to take his place. One thing the LGBTQ press missed or decided to ignore was that several gay porn stars died in mysterious ways around this time, all from alleged overdoses. In each case there were no follow up reports about what happened but there was no additional reports with any of the deaths that happened during this period.

More Truths

Multiple sources have confirmed that Dean actually died in September 2018. It wasn't until one reporter asked why he hadn't been in any more scenes that the story of his death broke. When asked why someone would want to kill the porn star, it was suggested that he was eyeing retirement from the industry.

There were also stories that he was about to come forward with his own #MeToo story. Sources haver been tight lipped about what he was going to reveal a producer had been forcing him to have sex with him in order to keep working. Another likely scenario was a costar may have forced him into having sex. Similar allegations had been made about the biggest male porn star, James Deen, so it would not be unheard of. With the female stars coming forward with their stories, it would have been the perfect time for a gay performer to share his story with the world as well. Dean would have been the perfect target with his desperation for cash, drug addiction, and perfect physique, for someone to take advantage of him. Even the threat of him coming forward would have been enough for a powerful person to want to silence him.

Adding to the theory that Dean knew his time in porn was up, fans have acknowledged he had set up an OnlyFans page. The website allows creators to connect with their fans and charge them for content. Most of the content is X-rated and the page that Dean set up was no different.

It may never be known what happened to Kyle Dean. His his life was cut tragically short. Will the family ever get answers about what happened to the young man they love?

Chapter Seven: Snack Attack

Snack Attack

Snack Attack

Has a trip to the store ever become a life-changing event? For Florida Man, Ryan Greenlee it certainly has. After a trip to Walgreens went sideways, he told a friend: "I didn't do nothing, all I wanted to do is go to the store, bro." This is something that could happen anywhere in the world but it felt like it had to happen in the Sunshine State.

While there have been many crimes that have happened in Florida, most of them were weird but in a very serious way. Greenlee's trip to the store, while serious, almost could be comical, even if it takes a dark sense of humor to laugh at it. Part of the reason the situation is so humorous is because of the motivation. Beef jerky.

Live From Walgreens

Social media has invaded every part of our lives. Even when we commit crimes, there is a pull to share it with the world. Now with each platform having a "Live" section, where a user uses their phone or computer camera to talk to followers in real-time, the pull to share more has increased considerably. Even the most mundane part of life is shared via the live option for some people.

Greenlee decided that he was one of the most interesting people around, and therefore people would want to see him during his everyday life. To that end, he live-streamed a trip to Walgreens on Wednesday, May 22, 2019. For the most part, there was nothing special about his decision to do this. Drag queens in New York City often do the same thing with a late-night trip to target. Greenlee's decision to live-stream his trip was a bit different. While the drag queens make dirty jokes and play with toys, Greenlee decided to get violent. Because beef jerky.

Blame It On The Beef Jerky

Once he was at the convenience store/pharmacy, Greenlee finally got his hands on two packages of beef jerky. In one of the more bizarre moments of the situation, he looked directly at the camera and waved his cash in front of it. Some have said it was something he did specifically for his Facebook audience. After the clerk rang up the merchandise, the total was read to him, as is customary with retail cashiers. The problem was that he didn't have enough money to pay for the snacks. A real problem for someone who really wanted the beef jerky.

Instead of putting one of the packages back or acting respectfully, Greenlee decided that it was the cashier's fault he didn't have enough money. As a rational person would expect his plan didn't work. This is where he took it to a physical level, he began throwing things at the cashier. The temper tantrum has been described as one that would be expected from a toddler.

As he was throwing things wildly, one of the items hit a two-month-old baby. Understandably, the mother of the child was irate that her child had been hit by the man-child. When she was interviewed by local media she explained: "I was just so angry that I didn't even cry, I was just trying to be as level headed as I could." The baby can be heard crying off camera but it didn't pick up the baby being hit by the flying object.

Another of the store's employees stepped in, trying to help diffuse the situation. It didn't help. It is unclear who called the cops, but they were contacted while the situation was unfolding. They were waiting for Greenlee once he walked out of the store.

Who knew beef jerky could create so much trouble?

Live Arrest and Charges

As Greenlee ran to the car, the camera began fuzzy and shaky. He told his friends that he did nothing wrong, despite the camera catching him throwing things at the clerks. On camera and social media, he continued to rage about the situation. He was very upset that he was not able to get his beef jerky. Officers wanted to speak to him, but there was no interest in that.

At some point, the camera was turned off and Greenlee was arrested in relative privacy. Still, he resisted arrest and began hitting the arresting officers. He now faces several charges including child abuse, battery of an officer of the law, resisting arrest, resisting arrest with violence.

Maybe beef jerky needs to be outlawed. At least in Florida.

Chapter Eight: Ketchup Cheating

Oh, Florida. What would the United States do

Ketchup Cheating Crime

Florida is home to Disneyworld and some of the weirdest, most bizarre crimes on record. It seems like criminals try to come up with ways to be crazier than the last one. Even the most simple things become some of the wildest and most talked about crimes. In some of the cases, there is nothing remotely logical about the situation.

Take the case of Peter Wagman. After he assaulted his girlfriend on June 2, 2019, he was placed under arrest. There are many people who think that what he did wasn't so bad. However, he did commit a crime and he certainly tried to out crazy the other Florida Men who have committed crimes. And he did so by using condiments.

Arguing, Cheating, and Ketchup Oh, My!

What kind of condiment would pair well with cheating rumors? Apparently, the answer to that is ketchup. While he was fighting with his long term girlfriend, she irritated him greatly. How? She went to bed in the middle of an argument they were having. This didn't sit well with Wagman. Especially since the argument stemmed from him accusing her of having an affair with an unnamed man and she told him that he had lost his mind.

Whether he was trying to prove her accusation or he thought this was a good idea, he went to the refrigerator. Many people would have thought he would have been getting a beer to cool off. That wasn't what Wagman had in mind though, he was angry and raring to finish this argument once and for all. After he grabbed the bottle of ketchup, he headed up the room he shared with his girl.

As the ketchup began covering his girlfriend's body, he screamed

"...that's what you get, bitch!'" Some people do use food as a way to enhance their sex life, and many thought this was the case between Wagman and his girlfriend. Even with the vulgar language, it could have been his way of making up with and seducing her. It could make sense in most cases.

This is not one of those cases, however.

A Side Of Charges Come With That

The unnamed girlfriend told police that she "woke up to ketchup being poured on her by the defendant." They took her statement and noted that there were still smudges of the condiment on her. The girlfriend was still shaken up while speaking with them, something that was noted in their report. Officers who came to the scene let the alleged criminal have his say as well.

He denied doing any such thing, as one would expect from a criminal. He suggested the ketchup was not poured on her and maybe she had dropped some on herself as she was eating dinner. However, the arresting officer didn't buy the excuse. The cop noted that there was ketchup on the "right side of his pants." Wagman said nothing about the evidence. But why would he? He may not have known it was there. Or he may have felt he had a good defense since he accused her of cheating on him. After all, who would convict a man who poured ketchup on a cheating woman?

Denial Excuses

He continued to deny that he did anything wrong. Though he did start admitting to them that if he had done, there was a reason for his actions. His girlfriend was cheating on him, this accusation was something that had been hurled at his girlfriend many times in their relationship. It was a big issue in their relationship. An issue that should have probably been resolved or ended it altogether.

Ending the relationship would have probably been better. Over the course of their 11-year relationship, each had been arrested and charged with domestic assault many times. Mostly when it happened they would spend one night in jail and then reconcile with one another. Much to their loved one's dismay. Most believed the couple was toxic and needed to get away from one another.

However, that didn't seem to be part of their plan. They must have believed themselves to be part of a beloved romantic comedy or something.

Comedy In The Condiments

There are those who believe that it is only a matter of time before

Saturday Night Live parodies this situation. There is comedy to be mined from what Wagman did. Maybe they should take out the part about him doing it as a punishment for the alleged cheating. But the rest of the story could be funny.

Is there too much sun in Florida and that's why people act so strange? Some have suggested that the reason some Floridians act oddly is that they think they will be called eccentric. However, when everyone is acting like lunatics, it does not mean one is eccentric. It makes the state as a whole seem like it has lost all common sense. Or maybe they just don't realize what a good relationship looks like?

In her hit song, "Never Really Over," Katy Perry talks about how hard it is to get over a bad relationship. She talks about how hard it is to let go of what was thought to be a forever love.

For Wagman though, the forever love would end because he poured ketchup on his girlfriend. A judge issued a restraining order against him, which is supposed to keep him away from his now ex-girlfriend. This was a unique case in most places.

But in Florida, it was just another day.

Chapter Nine: Nose Candy Denial

Cocaine Nose

Nose Candy Denial

"I didn't do it!" Children will argue with their parents, even if they are caught red-handed. One Florida man took immature denial to a whole new level, even as the police had concrete evidence that he was guilty. In the end, he was still arrested despite his denial and he had no one to blame but himself.

It all started when the police were attempting to make a routine pullover at 4:30 in the morning. At that time, drunk drivers can usually be found making their way home. Police will often patrol a little more as the bars close and drunks make their way to a restaurant for an early breakfast or attempt to drive home. Fabricio Tueros Jimenez was a passenger in the car. The police pulled over his friend. They noticed a white substance on Jimenez's nose, the 20-year-old answered with "it's not mine."

It's Not Mine

It shocked Jimenez that they believed it was cocaine and not a powder from a donut. In his mind, it could have even been powdered sugar. In the cop's defense, the suspect was blurry-eyed and he stumbled around when he was asked to get out of the car. They had more than enough evidence that it was an illegal substance. While his denials might have been amusing, there was no way the police were going to let him go quite so easily. A confession might have been a bit more subtle for the young man, but he did not see it that way and continued to deny that anything was amiss.

With more than enough probable cause, the police searched the car and Jimenez's person. What they found was beyond what any of them thought would be there. Along with the coke on his nose, police also found a small bag of cocaine, 250 grams of weed, and 13 Xanax pills on his body. There were more than enough drugs to arrest the young man and have him charged with possession. He continued to deny that any of what was found was his.

Not His First Snort

Just as a matter of due diligence, the police tested the substance on his nose. The test came back conclusive that it was cocaine. Jimenez was no stranger to drug charges, he had faced them in his past. He had been pulled over by police in August of 2018. The officer found a massive amount of drugs on his person and in the car. He was arrested and taken into jail.

With that case, he admitted the drugs were his. Theories were floating around that part of the reason he continued to deny the drugs were his in the more recent case was that he had violated his parole. In 2018, there was a lot of talk about how bad his attitude was. The jury found this to be off-putting and convicted the young man.

A judge was not amused by his antics. Despite the denials from Jimenez, the judge revoked his parole and he was sent back to jail. He is expected to finish the remainder of his original sentence. Many believe he will be taken from jail to rehab after being let out again.

But the drugs weren't his. At least in his mine.

Chapter Ten: The Hamburgular Strikes

The Hamburgular Strikes

The Hamburgular Strikes

When a craving hits, it needs to be satisfied. This was the case for one Florida Man, who needed to get his Frosty fix as soon as possible. Instead of waiting for the local Wendy's to open, he decided to open the restaurant himself. Some have blamed the chain for being so delicious. But why blame the victim?

Figuring out the motives behind this crime is not simple. Humans are complex creatures and they make decisions based on their needs in the heat of the moment. Hunger is a powerful motivator and can sometimes make people act differently than they normally would. Of course, since this took place in the Sunshine State, some believe there are different rules for them. It is up to each person to decide which is true.

In With A Brick

Protesters used bricks to fight back against the NYPD during the Stonewall Riots in 1969. Our Florida Man, who was never identified, must have taken inspiration from them as he used a brick to force his way into the Wendy's restaurant. While both were crimes, at least the protesters started a revolution. The Florida Man reinforced the notion that the crimes committed in the Sunshine State are crazy and out there.

After the brick went through the window and the Florida Man let himself into the Jensen Beach area restaurant, he decided to get some food. He got the grill going and threw a hamburger on it, and started making some fries. Some people have wondered why he didn't just take the money and leave. He was hungry and needed the sustenance to sustain himself.

Not The Only Robbery

Breaking into the restaurant and making food was not enough for our Florida Man. It generally never is. After he was finished eating, he went to the safe and took as much money as he could. When he left Wendy's he went to another restaurant and did the same thing in the other diner. There was no word on what kind of food he made for himself at the other restaurant but it's safe to assume it was something delicious. He must have figured the police were only a step or so behind him, so instead of taking the money from the safe, he took the whole thing with him. It saved him some time for sure.

After the first two successes, one would think that would be enough. However, our Florida Man was not content with leaving well enough be. He decided to try and rob a gas station. The third time was not the charm.

Giving him some time to get away is the fact that police can't seem to get their act together. Someone made a post on their social media accounts that confused Wendy's for McDonald's. A post on their Facebook page read: "A suspect coined as the modern-day Hamburglar doesn't appear to have any problem making himself right at home after breaking into local food establishments to make himself a burger." Our Florida Man was caught on camera committing these crimes and has evaded the police thus far.

Maybe he is frying up a hamburger right now.

Chapter Eleven: Share It On Facebook

Share Murder on Facebook

Share It On Facebook

It seems that Florida criminals take the "hold my beer" memes a bit seriously. A crime is reported about someone killing their spouse and the Floridian decides they must up the ante, it's not enough to commit the murder they have to do something bigger. There is one case though that originates in the Sunshine State that will be hard to top.

Derek Medina killed his wife, posted the picture on social media, and then called the police on himself. When asked why he posted the picture on Facebook, Medina responded that he wanted his in-laws to know their loved one was dead. And as people are fond of saying nowadays, "if it's not on Facebook, it's not official." This was his way of making it official that his wife was dead and that he killed her.

Romancing The Waitress

Jennifer Alfonso was a waitress at Denny's when she met Medina. He was one of her customers and began flirting with her. The pair hit it off right away and began dating shortly after they met. It seemed to be the forever kind of love that most people crave. It didn't seem to bother Alfonso that while she had a traditional job, her beau did not.

Medina was anything but a traditional career man. He seemed to throw things at the wall to see what would stick. To that end, he self-published some self-help books that didn't sell quite as well as he had hoped they would. He tried to be an actor but most directors weren't interested in working with him, with sources claiming it was because he had an attitude and not willing to take notes. He tried to be a social media influencer but was never able to amass enough of a following to get that career going. The one job he was good at and found some success with was being an amateur boxer. Despite the lack of career direction, Alfonso fell madly in love with Medina.

Just a month into their courtship, Alfonso and Medina were married. Many were surprised by the speed at which things had progressed but got swept up with the couple and were truly happy for them. Even Alfonso's daughter thought it was quite cute that her mom found a husband so quickly. For their honeymoon, they engaged in an activity that they both enjoyed, even as some of their loved ones gave them the side-eye.

They enjoyed chasing ghosts together, so they made that part of their honeymoon experience. Reports all talked about how the couple found this to be a great bonding experience and one of the very few things that they could agree on. David Ovalle wrote for the Miami Herald, "Her and Derek used to go see ghost tours in different cities." This would be one of the few times the couple smiled together.

Fighting And Toxicity

Married life did not agree with the couple. Outside of their ghost hunting trips, they fought like cats and dogs. Many people in their circle believed that divorce was imminent. "They would just fight about silly things, and he would break up with her often, he would throw her things to the side and insult her and then ignore her, Jen used to call them 'Mexican stand-offs.' She would surrender often. She loved him," Daysi Fernandez, who was Alfonso's best friend, would later tell reporters about the couple.

Those who believed divorce was inevitable were proven to be right, as Alfonso finally had enough of Medina and left him. She began to put her life back together, and move on from the dramatic relationship that had colored her life for so long. Her loved ones all talked about how happy and healthy she was during this period. It was music to their ears that she was doing so well and made them happy. It would not last forever.

Medina decided to reach out to his ex and ask for a second chance. She agreed to try to give their relationship another chance, with the hope that he had changed.

Almost immediately they began to fall back into familiar patterns. The same things they argued about before were fought about again, and this time the fight escalated into physical altercations. Jealousy fueled a lot of their fights. When Medina found out one of Alfonso's coworkers hit on her, he was not pleased. Fernandez recounted what he said, "'I'm gonna stay at Denny's with a gun outside and see if he's gonna [-- --] with me."

Despite this, the day after their divorce was finalized the pair remarried. Though Alfonso had her doubts that this was the right move for her to make.

Waking Up To Fight And Die

As the relationship once again deteriorated, Alfonso began to complain to friends that she was unhappy. She also confided that Medina's training as a boxer had been turned on her several times. "He was really like sick in the head, He would tell her things to make her sad or to scare her," Fernandez told reporters. Medina also used psychological warfare against his wife and would master it later on in his life.

Alfonso had an early shift on August 8, 2013, so she asked her husband to wake her up. Medina failed to do so, no one knows why he didn't wake her up. When she awoke, she was very unhappy with her husband. This led to another epic fight between the couple, and it became physical once again. "She started throwing things at him, just sort of like a typical type of fight that they would have," Ovalle wrote in one of his multiple reports on the case.

After the fight, she went downstairs and made breakfast for her 10-year-old daughter. Medina wasn't done with the argument though, and followed her downstairs and continued to yell and scream at her. Medina alleges his wife punched him in the chest, which resulted in his next action. He says it was self-defense.

However, the camera that had been put up disagrees with his assessment. He went back to their bedroom, upstairs. When he is seen on the camera again, there is a gun in his hand. In an effort to protect herself, Alfonso grabbed a knife but her husband was able to get it out of her hand with ease. Medina put the knife back into the drawer. Visibly angered, he shot his wife several times.

Alfonso fell to the floor dead. Her daughter was upstairs in her room during this entire situation.

Pics Or It Didn't Happen

Instead of calling the police, Medina took photos of his wife's body and started sending the pictures to people who loved Alfonso. One of the people who received the photo was his wife's best friend. "I thought that Jen was really playing some role in 'Walking Dead' or something. And I'm like 'All right, whatever, dude if that makes you happy,'" Fernandez was not believing her best friend had been killed, it was why she didn't call the police.

Once the texts were all sent, he happily posted the pictures on Facebook. He used the post to hint at what would become his eventual defense, that he had to protect himself from his wife. Here is the text of the post, unedited:

"Im going to prison or death sentence for killing my wife love you guys miss you guys takecare Facebook people you will see me in the news my wife was punching me and I am not going to stand anymore with the abuse so I did what I did I hope u understand me"

Family Man Self-Defense

Medina continued to claim the murder was self-defense despite the fact a camera caught everything that happened. Medina's lawyer, Saam Zangeneh, furthered the argument by admitting the relationship was volatile and adding that Medina felt the need to protect himself from Alfonso.

Medina and his lawyer tried to play up the family angle and tried to make him look like a good father figure for Alfonso's daughter. Their evidence was the fact that he told his stepdaughter to stay in her room and not to leave. Conveniently they left out the fact that the girl's mother was dead in the kitchen because she had been shot eight times.

Medina admitted to detectives that he shot his wife but claimed he was afraid of her. The investigators wondered why he would be scared of his wife. Especially seeing as he had a 25-0 record in the boxing ring. It didn't add up to them.

Medina further tried to make himself seem to be a good family man when he was asked why he uploaded the graphic pictures of his wife dead on the floor. His answer was "So the family would know and be notified and they can rush over there and get my stepdaughter." Calling someone to pick her up was not an option for him, apparently. Some have wondered if the real motivation was to try and reignite his social media influencer career.

"Ladies and gentlemen, the evidence will show that he emptied the clip, eight shots at Jennifer, causing 21 entry and exit wounds, And what did he do then? He did what people do when they win -- he told people about it. He took a picture of her and he posted it on Facebook," that was how the prosecutor summed up the case in the closing arguments. The jury found Medina guilty on all of the charges against him in just a few hours.

Conspiracy For Conviction

Medina was not happy with the conviction. As his team was working on the appeal, he had a sentencing hearing. It was during this hearing that he reached for the stars and upped his Florida man game.

Ignoring the fact that he confessed and had been caught on camera murdering his wife, he blamed the release of Universal Pictures movie Unfriended while he was on trial for the guilty verdict. The movie was a teen horror story that bore no resemblance to Medina's case. He wasn't finished with his new defense though, it was going to a national level.

He decided that because of the guilty verdict, he was given a fair trial. So he called on President Barack Obama to look into the corruption he was alleging, again the post is unedited from his actual quote:

"I will be suing this world, Not only that, Unfriended, the movie by Universal Pictures, came out with a movie before my trial, which was unfair. OK. Which was biased. And, um, pretty much the point I'm trying to make is that I did not get a fair trail. I will be taking action. I will be suing, and I want Barack Obama, president of the United of the States of America, to focus on corruption."

It seemed he was suing the world in an effort to help set up a way for him to appeal the case.

Crazy For Appeal

Proving the theory that Medina and his lawyers wanted to set up an appeal, Zangeneh began telling reporters that the defense had been banned from admitting evidence that would have exonerated his client. According to the defense lawyer, "We had photographs in her phone with regards to satanic rituals. There's a lot of things that we had that we wanted to introduce but the court limited our ability to educate the jury with regards to that." The video of Medina shooting Alfonso must be a minor inconvenience for them.

None of the arguments landed with Judge Yvonne Colodny. In fact, she turned Medina's words on his Facebook post against him, "You foretold your future, You wrote on Facebook that 'I am going to prison,' and that is where you will be going."

Colodny sentenced Medina to life in prison. He will need to serve at least 25 years before he will be eligible for parole.

So far, Medina has won the "hold my beer" competition. No one has even come close to being as out there with their crimes as he is.